Also by Rome Za

Awaken The Warrior Within

BAREHEARTED

My Journey With Vulnerability and Self Love

Rome Za

Copyright © 2019 by Rome Za.

All rights reserved. I support copyright. Copyright fuels creativity, promotes free speech, and creates a bright future for our culture. Copyright is the lifeblood for the artist. Thank you for buying an authorized edition of this book and for complying with copyright laws by not reproducing, scanning or distributing any part of it in any form without permission. Thank you for your support.

Front cover image by Alexandra Dobreva

First printing edition 2019

www.ROMEZA.com

For my children Alan and Leo

Forward

Dear Reader,

I am blessed to have been given the honor of writing this foreword... yet I am filled with my own self-doubt. As I try to gather my thoughts and arrange them into coherent patterns I struggle with my own vulnerabilities and insecurities. I have ventured out of my zone of comfort and the voice in my head can sense it. "What do you know about writing a foreword" it whispers. Fueled by every memory of failure, every time that someone made me feel like I wasn't enough, the voice grows louder. "Don't do it!" it hisses, growing desperate as I start to write. "Don't let Rome talk you into putting yourself out there like this." I grip my coffee cup for confidence and stumble on.

Why? Why am I choosing to do that which is uncomfortable as opposed to politely declining or offering some elaborate excuse? Well one reason is because I know that I can never have the extraordinary life I want if I act on the impulses of the scared child in my head. But there is another reason too.

The other reason is that I am inspired by the courage and vulnerability shown by Rome in the writing of this book and I am channeling some of that in my own writing. We are all highly social creatures. We decide what is and what is not possible based on the actions of others. As his best friend, I have always admired Rome's bravery. Whereas my own tendency is to first dip my feet into the ocean of the unknown, Rome dives in headfirst. I have watched him do this in every walk of life. From talking to girls as a teenager, to fighting competitors that outweighed him by 50 pounds in jiu-jitsu, to starting businesses as a young adult, to picking his family and up and moving from NYC to the unknowns of a beach town in

Costa Rica.

This spirit to lead by example, to do that which is difficult, is as much a part of who Rome is as the cells of his body. In the writing of this book, he has chosen to do what is most difficult for him (and probably for all of us.) He has lowered all of his defenses and shared with the world his weaknesses, his insecurities, his fears, and his doubts. In doing so, he lets us know that wherever we are in our journey, no matter how dark it may seem, we are not alone. This is his roadmap through the maze of emotions that we all must navigate at different points in our lives. I hope that reading each of these beautiful poems inspires you as much as it inspires me and gives you the courage to keep moving forward.

Mike Chulack

Chief Copywriting Officer

www.DrIanStern.com

READER,

Imagine for a moment...that you and a bunch of your friends are standing on a 10x10 plot of land that is quickly being surrounded by hot, molten lava. The only way out is to cross the lava river by hopping onto small rocks that protrude a few inches above it.

Everybody looks around. Then at each other. Waiting for somebody to go 1st.

And then, just like in the movies, everybody looks over and there is one person who is already on the 3rd rock out. Focused and leading the way.

I am grateful and fortunate that for a lot of things in my life, Rome is that person. The first to take the leap and show that the path is safe. And which not to follow.

I hope that through this book and these poems, Rome's courage in the face of vulnerability and raw emotion encourage you to look deeper and know that you are powerful and full of light. Even during the darkness.

Dimitry Godzin

Chief Marketing Officer

www.DrIanStern.com

Table of Contents

Introduction 1
Intention of this Book 4
How To Read This Book 5
1:. Time To Shine 6
2: Taking Everything To Heart 7
3: Surrender 9
4: Boiling Inside 11
5: Something More 12
6.: Living In Your Head 14
7: What Do You Want? 16
8: Darkness 18
9: You matter. 20
10: On Time 22
11: Talking To Myself 23
12: What is a feeling? 24
13: My Story 25
14: True Friends 27
15: Old School 29
16: The Game 30
17: Passed Down 31
18: Daily Choices 33
19: Rx 35
20: Vulnerable 37
21: Risking Love 38
22: Best Relationship Ever 40

23:	Super Stressed	42
24:	Scared to be a man	43
25:	What If?	44
26:	Play Full On	46
27:	Gratitude	47
28:	Great Advice	48
29:	Advice for living	50
30:	Modern Parenting	51
31:	Living Lighthouse	52
32:	The little voice that says I can	53
33:	Listen Deep	55
34:	Excuses	56
35:	The Gift of Fire	57
36:	Fire In My Veins	59
37:	Connected To Nature	60
38:	Opinions Of Others	61
39:	I Can't	62
40:	A Real Man	63
41:	Things That I Fear	67
42:	Gossip	69
43:	Heartbreak	70
44:	Dark and Light	71
45:	The Fighter	72
46:	Peter Pan Becomes a Man	73
47:	Darkness at my Doorstep	74
48:	Not Enough	76
49:	Heart Open	78
50:	The Past Is Gone	80

51: Hidden Gift 81
52: Life Gets Hard 83
The End… Or is it just the beginning? 86

Introduction

This book that you are holding in your hands right now contains countless breakdowns, battles with anxiety, depression, fear, feelings of unworthiness, and just overall darkness that I didn't know how to deal with.

I didn't know how to process these emotions. Emotional intelligence wasn't something I was taught growing up, and honestly I didn't even know that it existed.

I was only familiar with 4 emotions. Fear, Sadness, Anger and sometimes happiness (but very rarely.)

I ran away from these feelings for many years…

And they just kept coming back stronger, bigger, bad-der, and the suffering kept growing.

Then in May of 2019, it all came to a peak.

I was supposed to be having an incredible day, I finally got what I had wanted, but something felt very wrong and my suffering was greater than it ever was.

You see for the last 60 days we were selling our pet supplement company and I was in charge of all the negotiations and conversations with the buyers.

It was a very new experience for me that contained a lot of stress, lessons, and all the old culprits of not enoughness, and of course so much anxiety.

I just received a text message that the funds hit the account.

This was amazing!

It was official, I would finally be debt free.

We just sold our first multi-million dollar company.

I was sitting in my warm, empty bathtub listening to Peter Gabriel "Don't Give Up"

Sobbing, Crying, Feeling emptier than I had ever felt before, and I didn't know what to do.

The money didn't fill the void that I had inside of me, neither did the achievement…

This book is my journey on becoming whole again.

This book contains lessons, advice, breakthroughs and realizations that took me many years to get to.

This book can potentially hold the key for you to experience that suffering through my eyes and heart, and possibly learn from it so that you are prepared when the dark night of the soul will happen for you.

I always loved poetry as a kid, but I stopped allowing myself to write it very early because I always had a feeling of "not good enough" flowing through my veins.

I always felt like I was unworthy of being good enough at anything.

As if those that become famous authors or poets were chosen by the gods, and there was nothing that could be done about it.

As I am writing this I am 32 years old and I had a huge breakthrough,

I realized that I am worthy, I am enough, I am lovable & loving,

and I have qualities of GREATNESS pulsing through my veins as all the amazing Great men and women who came before me.

I am truly standing on the shoulders of giants and I am so grateful to all of my teachers, Mentors, coaches, and friends that have inspired me to write this book that you are holding in your hands right now.

INTENTION OF THIS BOOK

For the last 10 years of doing this work, people have told me they wish they had a mini Rome that they could put in their pocket to help them get empowered and inspired when times got dark.

My intention for this book is to help you break free of the cultural ideas about who you are, how you should feel, what you should do, and how you should live.

In order to create the life of your dreams, you WILL go through growing pains.

My intention for this book is to provide you with a flashlight for the tunnel of darkness that you are either going through right now or that you are sure to go through in the future, IF YOU CHOOSE to stay with it and keep walking forward.

I wrote this book to help you tap into your heart and FEEL again (or even for the first time in your adult life.)

I love you.

I wish for you a life that you might have not had the courage to wish for yourself just yet.

I believe in you.

You are worthy.

You are lovable.

You are destined to play a bigger game.

You are not alone on this journey.

You are resilient.

You are powerful beyond measure.

How To Read This Book

I wrote this book with the intention of walking alongside you on this journey of life.

We all go through different struggles at different times in our lives, and each poem was written to connect to different phases of your life as it contains the flashlight to illuminate the tunnel of darkness you might be walking through right now.

These poems can be used as something to contemplate during your journaling or your meditations, I wrote them with you in mind.

You can read this book straight through and then return to each poem that really connected with you in the moment, or you can take your time and read 1 poem per day and meditate on them, or you could do both.

Either way, take your time, chew it in small bites and make sure that it digests inside of you.

So grab a journal, a pen, a highlighter, some citrus essential oil and use this book to help you create a new experience of feeling in your life.

Let's dive in together!

1.

TIME TO SHINE

They say you can't do it,

They ask who you think you are?

They say with your skills you'll never go too far,

But I think it's time to show them,

I think it's time to shine,

Believe in yourself,

Take it one step at a time,

And before you know it,

It will be your time to shine!

2.
TAKING EVERYTHING TO HEART

Taking everything to heart,

Is how I learned to interact,

From the start.

Getting Angry,

Holding onto resentment,

Is where I got my discontentment.

Focus was inward,

Woe is me,

How can they do this?

What don't they see?

Getting riled up,

Getting emotional,

Broken Relationships,

Pain non-negotiable,

Sitting in my emotions,

Spiraling down,

Acting like an angry clown.

Losing control,

Feeling anxiety,

Losing trust in myself,

And my spontaneity.

Why am I acting,

like I am delirious?

Solution,

is not mysterious,

Time to remind myself,

It's not so serious,

Time to step up and be a man,

Time to stop throwing tantrums,

I am not Peter Pan.

3.

SURRENDER

Surrender is not a word that came naturally to me,

I thought it meant,

Giving up, running away, and quitting you see,

My whole life I've been fighting,

Mostly with myself,

Lashing out at my insecurities,

Ruining my health,

But then One day I realized,

That I am my greatest foe,

And I am the one who is stopping,

Stopping me to grow,

I started to look at surrender,

As a way to be,

It allowed me to let go,

It allowed me to be free,

The more that I surrendered,

The lighter that I felt,

The blockages removed,

The more holes on my belt,

The space that I'm creating,

Is to be more of me,

Surrender,

Vulnerability,

Now I'm finally feeling free.

4.

BOILING INSIDE

The anger that I'm feeling,

Has nothing to do with you,

It's what I'm dealing with inside,

It's my dark point of view.

I need you to hold space,

And be loving with me,

I am dealing with my darkness,

My insecurity.

I am battling inside,

between the dark and the light,

Not realizing that there is no need to fight.

They are both 2 parts of a whole,

Once I integrate my shadow,

I take control of my soul.

5.

SOMETHING MORE

Feel like you're here,

For something more?

Feel like It's right behind,

The magic door?

Like this feeling,

You can't ignore?

But you can't seem,

To get yourself,

Right off the floor?

Some days inspired,

Most days you're tired,

Wish you'd get fired,

Or one day hired,

Self love required,

Current situation,

Undesired.

Time to get what you desired,

Time to stand in the fire,

Its OK to perspire!

Time to step into your dream,

I know the evidence is unseen,

But you are here for more,

Countless adventures are in store,

Life no need to be a bore,

Time to get what you adore,

Tap into your valour,

Waters are going to get choppy,

Stay focused,

Don't get sloppy,

When life hits you,

Stand your ground,

Time to hear,

That winning sound!

You deserve it,

Say it loud,

Your dreams are yours,

You are endowed!

6.

LIVING IN YOUR HEAD

O you are so smart,

You are disconnected from your heart,

Everything should be logical,

Tapping in and vulnerability is illogical,

Everything is numbers,

Your heart is in a state of slumber,

Life is filled with doing,

Yourself you are just screwing,

Nothing feels fulfilling,

Soul you are just killing,

Life is feeling broken,

Consciousness not woken,

Days are filled with worry,

Nothing in a state of hurry,

Waiting for life to happen,

Refusing to just tap in,

Focus is always inward,

Spirit is feeling injured,

Time to make a shift,

Get out of the drift,

Focus needs to go out,

Then there will be no doubt,

Who you are at the core,

And what you are here for.

Get to be of service,

No more feeling nervous.

Tap into your purpose,

Stop living on the surface.

7.

What Do You Want?

What do you want,

To create in your life?

Is it misery, loneliness,

Struggle, and fights?

Is it connection, abundance,

Love and light?

You know it's your choice,

What you create in this life!?

You get what you ask for,

No fear to ask more,

Time to look inside,

And explore.

Time to spread your wings,

And soar!

Time to sing your war cry,

And ROAR!

Time to create,

What you are here for!

Time to share your love,

And be who you are,

At your core!

8.

Darkness

When the darkness takes over,

It feels like there is nowhere to go,

It's time for survival,

It's time to go below,

Below is where all my demons,

Live and talk to me,

Below is where my fears live,

Below is where I'm not free.

I feel the urge to lash out,

I feel the urge to hurt,

But the more conscious part of me,

Tells me to avert,

It tells me that this persons hurting,

And it tells me that I'm real,

It tells me that there's no need,

To make this person squeal.

Yes there are emotions,

That I get to sit and feel,

It's part of the human experience,

It's part of the whole deal.

When I feel emotions,

I let them pass through me,

Because If I hold onto them,

I will never be free.

9.

YOU MATTER.

You are important.

You are loved.

You are powerful.

You are beautiful.

You are special.

I love you. ♥

Sometimes I am feeling all alone,

Those times I don't want to pick up the phone,

At times I want to disappear,

Those times I am feeling all the fear,

Those times I tend to not see clear,

It feels like it could last for years,

The pain inside it gets severe,

My friends they reach out,

they are sincere,

But I don't want them to interfere,

So I get angry when they come near,

I start to spiral real real low,

I forget everything that I know,

I forget how I am full of love,

I forget I was sent from up above,

I forget how important I am to others,

I forget my brothers,

I forget my lover.

10.

ON TIME

Show up on time,

Never be late,

Whether its a meeting,

Or even a date,

People are watching,

People relate,

Step into leader,

Step into great.

11.

TALKING TO MYSELF

People say you're crazy,

When you talk to yourself.

We all do it daily,

We don't need no help,

It's important words are chosen,

That empower you.

Talking to yourself,

Is what you want to do.

Your mind is recording,

All the words that you use,

Moment by moment,

Make sure you don't abuse,

Plant the seeds daily,

Of empowerment,

Get rid of phrases like,

I can't, I wish, I'm spent.

12.

WHAT IS A FEELING?

What is a feeling,

But a passing gift?

Sadness and anger,

We allow to cause a rift.

Happiness,

Joy,

We hold on real tight,

Not realizing,

Eventually they'll bite!

Sit down and feel,

What passes through you,

And with time,

You will,

Gain a clue,

Of what the problem is,

And what you can change,

Run away though,

And you stay in your cage.

Get in front of your emotions,

And the whole world becomes your stage.

13.

MY STORY

My story is being written,

My tongue will not be bitten,

I will show up as who I am,

Not Johnny, Jack or Sam.

I will create from deep within my heart,

I lacked the courage to do it from the start,

I lacked the courage to be just who I am,

I showed up as all these other men,

Masks I wore,

Plastic like Ken.

I was scared of what they would say,

Criticism would ruin my day,

Life was just a silly play,

And I had my part,

I played it right from the very start.

But now the play is over,

Its time to start life over,

Figure out just who I am,

Claim my power as a man.

Stop the childish games,

Like Peter Pan,

Become more of myself,

Expand on my health,

Create more wealth,

Give back to others,

Mothers, sisters, brothers,

I am finally free,

Free to be me.

14.

True Friends

Friends show up,
And friends support,
Friends listen to you,
They don't retort.
Friends give back,
And friends they listen.
When you win,
They don't hate,
Their hearts glisten.
When things are rough,
Friends are there,
If you have cancer,
They will give their hair.
Friends love you,
Even when you don't.
Friends know your secrets,
Friends won't tell.
Friends will pick you up,
If you fell.
Friends got your back,

When things are scary.

They give the shirt off their back,

Even if their beliefs are contrary.

Friends know your fears,

Friends wipe your tears,

Friends work through conflict,

They don't disappear.

15.

OLD SCHOOL

Say hello to that person,

You pass by in the street,

Pick your eyes up and smile,

Don't look down on concrete,

Share your meal with someone,

We all deserve to eat.

Hold that door for that person,

Don't be so discreet.

Give your seat up to that lady,

And stand on your feet.

Call your friends and family,

Never mistreat.

Smile and stay resilient,

Even when thrown in the heat.

Be a man or woman who stands tall,

In defeat.

16.

THE GAME

Don't judge the player,

Don't judge the game,

Choose your experience,

Let go of shame.

Don't judge yourself,

Let go of blame.

Take responsibility,

That's why you came.

17.

PASSED DOWN

We are taught not to give,

Not to forgive.

We are taught to relive,

The mistakes that we made,

The memories fade,

But the debts are not paid,

We live all afraid,

Feeling betrayed,

Living in shade,

So we try to persuade,

Others to like us,

But it's all a masquerade,

We put on a show,

All out of flow,

Stagnate,

Don't grow,

Like a grenade,

Waiting to blow.

The answer is no,

When the question is life,

The feeling is trife.

We continue waiting,

Put off creating,

Spend our days hating,

Life energy fading,

While we are debating,

When to jump in.

We are scared of losing,

But even more to win.

We feel undeserving,

Like to win is a sin,

We avoid our true journey,

Like we shouldn't have been.

18.

DAILY CHOICES

Everyday is a choice,

Do I hear my own voice,

Amidst all the noise?

Do I give it my all?

Do I play it safe and small?

Do I face all my fears?

Through all of the tears…

Do I keep going on?

Even after I've won…

Do I keep testing self?

Or do I go on the shelf?

Life could be great,

Let go of the weight,

Let go of the hate,

Straighten up my gait,

Belief systems update.

Embracing my fate,

Tapping into innate,

Everyday I create,

Never showing up late.

Making my choice,

And spreading my voice.

19.

Rx

The body is our god given tool,

He who denies it,

Is a fool.

The body is one with mind,

To separate them,

You'll be left behind.

It's important to move it everyday,

It's important to move it,

Or you will pay.

Pain, suffering and disease,

Can be the future,

If you can't make the body,

Your expertise.

Give it daily what it needs,

Real food,

Sleep and bend the knees.

Move it slow,

And move it fast,

No one cares if you are last,

Yes it's normal to be gassed,

Don't compare and don't contrast,

If you move,

You will outlast.

Move it,

Move it,

Move it now,

You'll be blessed,

And well endowed.

Your body's flow,

Will now allow,

To live at one,

With the eternal tao.

20.

Vulnerable

Standing naked in the dark,

Arrows flying at their mark,

Open hearted,

Eyes are closed,

Gripping at a piece of clothes,

Inner voices come to blows,

Always fighting off my foes,

Suddenly, I realize I'm safe,

I'm the archer in this strafe,

I'm the bandit in this case,

Looking blankly in his face,

I create some loving space,

Give myself a warm embrace,

Critical thoughts,

I will replace.

Remind myself I am an ace,

That this is really a safe space.

21.

RISKING LOVE

My lips are shaking,

My legs are too,

I'm scared as hell,

I'm scared of you.

I'm scared you'll hurt me,

I'm scared you'll lie,

I'm scared that I will want to die.

I'm scared you'll laugh,

I'm scared I'll cry,

I'm scared if we fall in love,

One of us will die.

I'm scared i'll love you,

And mess it up.

I'm scared the real me,

is not enough.

I'm scared you'll treat me o' so rough,

I'm scared my heart has had enough,

I'm scared you'll reveal the real me,

I'm scared I'm not who I'm supposed to be.

I take a deep breath,

Put one foot forward,

My body moves a little bit toward,

Toward a big risk,

I'm going to take,

A risk that might reveal I'm fake.

But without risk there is no reward,

A great life you just can't make,

Without moving forward.

So with my legs and lips that shake,

I walk towards you,

This risk i'll take.

22.

Best Relationship Ever

Say you are giving it your all,

But honestly you are playing small,

Never show emotion,

Relationships in erosion,

No one really knows you,

Feelings and thoughts never show through,

Everything feels scripted,

Truth inside encrypted,

Connection is restricted.

No one will ever get in,

Showing vulnerability is a sin,

Break ups regularly you take on the chin,

In your life,

Love will never win.

Until you learn to open up,

When the pain will be enough,

For you to be woken up.

Once you learn to tap in,

Get out of the cage you are trapped in,

Take the shell off your heart,

That its wrapped in,

Time to expose you,

Until your loved ones know you,

Show them who you are,

Yes you are bizarre,

No they won't run far,

Because you truly are a superstar!

23.

Super Stressed

Overwhelmed,

Feeling stressed,

Things not going as I planned,

Look around,

Scowled face,

Looking for someone to blame.

Heating up,

Turning red,

Feeling like I'm losing the game.

Took a breath,

Slowed it down,

Finally letting go of shame.

Caught myself,

Write it down,

Letting go of the pain.

Feeling clearer,

Shed the fearer,

Finally the peace has really came.

24.

SCARED TO BE A MAN

Scared to be a man,

Fear is out of hand,

Looking for a way,

Angry yes I may.

Scared to take the lead,

Fear to do the deed,

Choking what I say,

Fear leads the way.

No trust in myself,

Scared to make the wealth,

Feeling unaccepted,

All of life affected,

Health and joy neglected.

Anxiety taking over,

Life is good as over.

25.

WHAT IF?

Feeling unaccepted,

Relationships neglected,

Start to hate all others,

Fathers, sisters, brothers.

Giving of myself,

Cant enjoy my wealth.

Starting to resent,

Confidence has went.

Cup is feeling empty,

Resentments are a plenty,

Start to hate myself,

Losing all my health,

My life is full of fear,

The end is finally near.

Full of all regrets,

Can't pay all my debts,

Scared to take the risk,

Nothing like Wilson Fisk,

Dying all alone,

Empty in my home,

Gave up all my power,

Even in the final hour.

Life could have been great,

If only I had some faith,

Trusted in myself,

Created real wealth,

Minded to my health.

Looked deeper in myself,

Gave instead of taking,

Stopped all of the faking,

O' what could have been,

Had I chose myself to win!

26.

Play Full On

Show up early,

Play full on,

Give it your all,

Remember to have fun.

Everyone is waiting,

For you to step into power,

Time is ticking away,

It's almost the final hour.

Leave it all in the arena,

Give your one hundred percent,

Win, lose or draw,

Never knees bent.

Stand up straight and wipe your tears,

You already won,

You conquered your fears.

27.

GRATITUDE

Gratitude is a feeling that everyone deserves to feel,

It can be for a flower,

Or even a meal.

We get caught up wishing,

Only a little more,

Missing the abundance,

Living only for what's in store.

We have many blessings,

Things we can acknowledge,

Life doesn't start when you graduate college.

We all have something we want to achieve,

But suffering while you get it,

You behave like a thief.

Remember to be grateful for the things that are there,

And more will be created,

For you to abundantly share.

28.

GREAT ADVICE

I listened to all the people,

That gave me "great advice",

They told me to stay in my lane,

Never try something twice.

I wanted their acceptance,

So I did as they say,

But then I realized,

It was a sad little play.

All the advice that they gave me,

It was all a lie,

I came so close to letting my own spirit die.

Now it's time for greatness,

Now it's time for power,

Serving the world on fire,

Like it's my final hour.

They said to be a doctor,

They told me to go to college,

I hated it the whole time,

Resented all the knowledge.

Then I took a risk,

Decided to leave it all,

I thought it would be better,

To make my own call.

At first it was real scary,

A bit exciting too,

But those that really risk it,

They find out all the clues.

Life is a journey,

Filled with twists and turns,

Follow your own heart,

Enjoy all the little burns.

Eventually you will make it,

And when you really do,

All the twists and turns

Will come together like glue.

29

ADVICE FOR LIVING

Wake up bright and early,

Wake up with the sun,

Eat organic produce,

Be patient with everyone.

Take time daily to hydrate real well,

Scrub your body daily,

So there's no funky smell.

Sit in meditation,

Or you can even walk,

Say nice things to others,

Or do not even talk.

Move your body daily,

Move it with some play,

Give it all you've got.

Now that's what I call a day.

30.

MODERN PARENTING

Today I woke up early,

To see you do your thing,

But what I noticed first,

Was your attention on the ping.

I tried to say good morning,

I tried to give you hugs,

But your attention was elsewhere,

Your phone and coffee mug.

So I decided to show you,

That I can be just like you,

I grabbed a phone and juice box,

But made a little boo boo.

That got your attention,

You got really mad,

You told me I was careless,

That I am being bad,

All I wanted was acceptance,

A little bit of love,

But you were busy scrolling,

Connecting with the wi-fi above.

31.

LIVING LIGHTHOUSE

Standing proudly up above,
Shining out your glowing love,
When the trouble does arise,
Your light illuminates the skies,
You deliver wisdom-knowledge,
Though you never finished college,
Giving love with open hands,
Never forcing with commands,
Letting others make own choice,
Living compassionately is your voice.

32.

THE LITTLE VOICE THAT SAYS I CAN

The thing that I am scared of,

Is the thing that I need.

The mean little voice,

Is the one that I heed,

Ironically though,

It's the one that impedes.

That voice stops me from my dreams,

It makes me question my team,

Makes me glisten,

Not gleam.

That voice has led me astray,

So much that I started to gray,

So much I started to pray,

So much I started to say,

Life isn't all it's cracked up to be,

Maybe this small life is god's plan for me,

No! It can't be,

I know it can't be,

My dreams are too big to play small,

It's time to stand tall,

It's time to get up every time that I fall,

It's time to trust and move forward,

It's not time to stall.

It's time to listen to the real quiet voice,

The one that says that I can,

That tells me that I am a powerful man.

That I can accomplish anything,

That I ever plan.

It's time for me to take a stand,

It's time for me to think more grand,

It's time for me to lend a hand.

It's time for me to ignore the fear,

It's time for me to wipe my tears,

It's time for me to listen deep,

To the little voice that is just a peep.

33.

LISTEN DEEP

What will they say,

Is my biggest fear.

When I fail at my task,

Is that all they will hear?

So I learn to play small,

Never stand tall,

Head looking down,

I never even look at the ball.

All because of my little fear,

My little fear of what they will hear.

34.

EXCUSES

Excuses come a dime a dozen,

You can hear them from your mom or cousin,

You can hear them all around,

But excuses are just a silly sound,

Excuses pose a grave danger,

They can even turn off a complete stranger,

Excuses keep you very small,

Excuses keep you down when you fall.

So give up all of your excuses,

Tap into your sacred muses.

Start movings towards the goal,

And remember when you fall,

Even if you have to crawl,

To get up, smile, and stand tall!

Because you're worth it after all!

35.

THE GIFT OF FIRE

Be mindful of your fire,

Always keep it hot,

But make sure the stones are around it,

To keep it in one spot.

Fire can keep you warm,

Fire can keep you fed,

But lose control of it,

And everything will be dead.

You can create abundance,

Or you can destroy the world.

The fire is your gift,

It can keep you out of the cold.

Make sure you learn to use it,

To benefit those in need,

Never to abuse it,

Only for good deeds.

Take care of your fire,

Always keep it lit,

Always show up honest,

Vulnerable,

And legit.

36.

Fire In My Veins

Fire on my back,

Stars in the sky,

Ready to live full on,

Not just waiting to die.

I am one with nature,

She is one with me,

I live my life connected,

Blessed as I can be.

37.

CONNECTED TO NATURE

Spend time in nature,
Hear her beautiful sounds,
She is saying softly,
Her love for us unbound.
Take in all the fragrance,
Breathe in all the love,
This was god's creation,
Filled with the stars above.

38.

OPINIONS OF OTHERS

They said I was too small,

They said I was too stupid,

They said never will he be a target for cupid,

For years that I believed them,

For years I played life scared,

Not taking my shot,

I thought everyone cared.

But then everything shifted,

I realized the lies,

Those people are just scared,

No more compromise,

It's time to really show them,

Who I truly am,

It's time to step into the infinite courageous man.

39.

I Can't

I didn't believe I could do it,

I didn't think I was that good,

Others told me never!

Never that you could,

For a long time I believed them,

I was playing small,

But now my mind has shifted,

Finally standing tall.

I create abundance,

Everywhere I go,

I let go of those fears,

I surrendered to the flow.

Now that I stepped into,

The man that I could be,

The naysayers are quiet,

I am finally free.

40.

A Real Man

A real man knows when to take a stand,

A real man always lends a hand,

A real man knows not to wallow,

Criticism and self doubt he'll never swallow.

A real man knows how to love,

Respect for all the creatures and the gods above.

A real man knows how to fight,

With him he carries all the dark and light.

A real man protects those that are weaker,

A real man continues to be a seeker,

A real man rises to the challenge,

He can work with his hands and is emotionally balanced!

A real man can cry,

Or laugh out loud,

A real man isn't scared to tell his son that he's proud.

A real man takes pride in pleasing his woman,

He is always present,

And gets up after losing.

A real man can fix his home,

A real man has the courage to be alone,

When hardships arise he doesn't bitch and moan,

He pushes through with a smile,

Courage to enroll others if he can't do it alone.

A real man is a leader,

He jumps right in,

Playing at 100,

He is looking for the win/win.

A real man in my eyes is many things,

When he accepts who he is,

He will grow his wings.

A real man can fight,

And love,

And struggle,

A real man inspires others,

He doesn't hide in a bubble.

A real man sings,

And a real man plays,

A real man can get lost writing poetry for days.

A real man makes money,

A real man creates,

A real man never shows up late for his dates.

A real man trusts others,

And especially himself,

He inspires the world,

And shares in his wealth.

A real man keeps his word,

A real man never says he's bored.

A real man has discipline,

A real man has love,

A real man has connection and faith in the heavens above.

A real man embraces his power,

A real man can stop and smell a flower,

A real man is comfortable in his own skin,

A real man doesn't cry when he fails to win.

A real man has courage,

A real man takes risks,

He always does the right thing,

He is no Wilson Fisk.

A real man is handy,

He creates with his hands.

A real man is not a wallflower,

He gets up to dance.

A real man gives back to those he can help,

A real man is confident,

He doesn't write negative reviews on yelp.

A real man supports other men on his path,

He always thinks abundant,

And remembers to laugh.

A real man stands tall in the face of defeat,

A real man doesn't cower,

He lives on his feet.

A real man takes care of his health,

A real man knows that his true wealth.

A real man chooses,

He doesn't live like a slave.

A real man is wild,

He doesn't always behave.

A real man is connected,

A real man is funny,

A real man knows he is not his money.

A real man speaks no lies,

A real man allows himself to cry when saying goodbyes.

A real man never quits,

But he is always surrendered,

A real man's actions will always be remembered.

A real man is at home in nature,

He can hunt, fish and forage,

But respect for mother earth,

Is something that's encouraged.

This real man is who I aspire to be,

Being a wholehearted man is the choice for me.

41.

THINGS THAT I FEAR

Sometimes I fear,

Losing it all,

Losing my mind,

And taking a fall.

Sometimes I fear,

I can't stand tall,

Pressure too much,

Ready to bawl.

Sometimes I'm angry,

Angry at you,

Don't know what to say,

Don't know what to do.

Sometimes I hate,

The moon and sun,

What have I done?

Who I've become.

Then I remember,

Why I am here,

All of my gifts,

Through all of the tears.

All of my stumbles,

All of my fears,

I pick my head up,

I put on a smile,

Remind myself,

Just one more mile.

Time to get moving,

Time to give back,

World is in need,

Of all of that.

42.

GOSSIP

People gossip,

People hate,

People hope you show up late,

People tell you,

You can't do,

People just don't have a clue.

They don't know inside your heart,

Target clear,

Hit like a dart,

Pay no mind to all the talk,

Head up high,

Time to walk the walk.

43.

Heartbreak

Sometimes I'm feeling oh so stressed

Sometimes I'm feeling emptiness,

At times I want to run and hide,

Sometimes I feel I can't confide.

Sometimes I want to lay and cry,

Sometimes it feels like I will die.

I thought that we will stay together,

But learning no,

Made my heart shatter.

I wondered deeply if I was a man,

I wondered if I still can,

I questioned all of my beliefs,

I felt like I had met a thief,

To see my own heart disappear,

All I had room for was the fear.

44.

Dark and Light

Daily movement,

Daily silence,

Inner peace,

To control violence.

Acceptance of my dark and light,

Know myself,

No need to fight.

45.

THE FIGHTER

Face in the dirt,

Tears in my eyes,

Everyone laughing,

Pain in my thighs,

They say it's over,

I say they lie,

It's my time to show them,

Not yet goodbye.

I crawl to my feet,

Put my hands up,

Flash them a smile,

Time to put up,

Give it my all,

I pull out a win,

Quitting for me,

The greatest sin!

46.

PETER PAN BECOMES A MAN

I do what I want,

I do what I please,

I live life standing,

Not down on my knees,

I stand for freedom,

I stand for life,

I pull out chairs,

I love my wife.

I take the time to inspire others,

I live like a man.

My word is my bond,

I am not peter pan!

47.

Darkness at My Doorstep

When the darkness comes,

I will stand tall,

I will show my teeth,

I will not bawl,

I will dig my heels in,

I am ready to brawl.

It will not pull me down to hell,

I've been there,

I know the smell.

I will not give up,

Never ring no bell,

I will keep showing up,

Even if I fell.

I will get up,

I will give it my all,

I will fight hard,

I will stand tall,

I will continue to fight,

Till my last breath.

I will keep growing,

Until my death.

48.

NOT ENOUGH

Some days I feel I am not enough,
These days are spent feeling rough,
I sit and analyze my life,
And wallow in the petty strife.
It takes me days to get unblocked,
Those days I struggle,
Those days I'm locked.
The thoughts are angry,
The thoughts are shame,
Some days I wish I didn't have a name.
But then I reach out,
And do some good,
I tap into kind-heartedness,
And brighten my mood.
I take care of myself,
And eat good food,
I remember now,
I'm a good dude.
I remember now I am enough,
I remember now I am real tough,

I remember now I love myself,
I remember now I AM the wealth!

49.

Heart Open

Keep your heart open,

No matter the pain,

Every moment is different,

It's never the same.

Let go of expectations,

Of how it should be,

Step into the moment,

And let yourself free.

The pain and the fear,

And the sadness too,

All brings a lesson,

A lesson to you.

But the lesson is there,

If you let yourself feel,

If you continue to run,

It will continue to steal.

Moments of life,

Of joy,

Of sorrow,

Acknowledge it now,

And enjoy tomorrow.

50.

The Past Is Gone

The Past is gone,
Just like the wind,
Yet we keep holding on,
To let go of it,
Is what we need,
Weighing on us like a ton.
To walk through life,
with all this baggage,
We forget to have any fun.
We kick ourselves,
And beat ourselves,
For what we have done.
Life is short,
The past is done,
It's time to create a new,
It's time to be,
It's time to dream,
Let go of feeling blue.

51.

HIDDEN GIFT

My whole life,

I hide my gift.

To cheap to share,

Shop in thrift,

To scared to show,

My heartfelt flow,

Scared of the critics,

I refuse to glow,

But now it's time,

It's time to go,

To show the world,

To not be low,

It's time to give,

My rhythm,

Flow.

It's time to break out,

off the shell,

It's time to leave,

My self made hell,

It's time to step,

into my courage,

It's time to take,

My gift out of storage,

It's time to give It,

all I've got,

To live this life,

Only one shot!

52.

LIFE GETS HARD

When it gets hard,

What do you do?

Do you quit?

Or do you push through?

DO you shut down?

And run and hide?

Or do you double up your efforts,

Hold on tight and go for a ride.

Life gets messy,

And life is hard,

Its guaranteed,

you will leave here scarred.

People will yell,

And some might hate you,

But it's only for a little,

When you succeed,

They will want to date you!

So when life starts to fight,

And you start to struggle,

Its only to help you grow,

And get you out of your bubble.

Give you perspective,

Your not defective,

At times get reflective,

But keep pushing on.

The struggle is real,

Or as real as you make it,

If it's getting too much,

Reach out to a friend,

Don't smile and just fake it.

People care about you,

More than you know,

Your mission in life,

Is to continue to grow,

With growth comes pain,

And sometimes we struggle,

Life gets intense,

And we all have to juggle,

Life might knock us down,

And kick us out of our bubble,

But remember if you're ever in trouble,

That I am here as a friend,

A support,

And some muscle.

And together we stand to solve this puzzle.

The End... Or is it Just the Beginning?

We are in this together, your struggles are my struggles.

Your love is my love.

Your pain is my pain.

Your wins are my wins.

Your losses are my losses.

I know we might not have met, but you inspire me!

You inspire me because through all of the hardships that you have gone through in your life, you are still showing up, and you are still playing this game of life.

The definition of INSPIRE that resonates with me is to "Breath life into..."

If this aligns with you, read this passage and conclusion to this book of poetry as if YOU co-wrote it with me, because in a way you did.

I have been trying to write a book for the last three years and I was blocked.

I would start writing it and then the voices from the past kept coming up...

"I am not enough"

"Who's going to read your poems?"

"People will see you as the fraud that you are"

"What gives you the right to write poetry anyways? Who do you think you are?"

"What will people say about you after reading your silly book of poetry?"

For three years this cycle would continue...

1. I would have an incredible experience and get super pumped up to write a book...

2. I would make an outline.

3. Sit down, start writing.

4. And by the time I had written around 20%, I would buy into the internal demons that would start to make me doubt myself, drag me down, and get me to take on another project.

This continued for three years!

Three years I battled myself.

Three years I muffled my heart from singing.

Three years of beating the shit out of myself on a daily basis.

Three years of battling between I can do this and I am not good enough to do it.

Then one day I had a breakthrough, it was a real "eureka" moment to say the least!

I realized that the self-doubting voices will probably never go away, and that's OK!

Most people have doubts.

Most people struggle with not feeling enough at times.

And most people (me included) allow those doubts to take over and keep US playing small.

The breakthrough was this...

My ego wants me to play small because it is a place that feels comfortable and safe.

It's a place where I produce just ENOUGH results to wow some people, but stay out of the beaming lights of criticism.

It's a place that I get to live in that EVERYONE likes me and the persona that I have built.

But that place doesn't work for me anymore.

I don't want to play small.

I don't want my life to be dictated by my emotions.

I don't want to produce just what I need to produce.

I want my life to be guided by intention, so no matter how I feel when I wake up, and no matter the circumstance, I will still show up in service to the world.

I want to ask god/universe for more and co-create it.

I want to be an inspiration for those people in my life that are watching me, because I CAN!

I want to empower others and lead the way courageously.

I realized that I was playing small and its not working anymore for me, my friends and family, and the rest of the entire world.

In my heart I have a gift to share and I want to give it all away to the wonderful souls that cross my path in life.

To me reading is a very intimate activity that I get to do, because it is a conversation that goes on inside of me with another souls ideas, that I don't have to seek

approval for, and I can interpret it anyway that I want.

Thank you for spending your time with me in one of the most intimate ways known to man.

My heart and soul goes out to you on this journey and I truly hope one day we get to meet, connect and create inspiration in this world together.

Thank you for taking this journey of self-discovery and self-expression with me...

I know this might sound crazy, and woo-woo, but I believe our lives have intersected for a specific reason...

I believe that there are no coincidences in this universe.

As the great Ram Dass said "We are all just walking each other home..."

www.ingramcontent.com/pod-product-compliance
Lightning Source LLC
LaVergne TN
LVHW041548070426
835507LV00011B/981